D0754701

NO LONGER PROPERTY
OF ANYTHINK
RANGEVIEW LIBRARY
DISTRICT

Diwali

Festivals Around the World

Words in **bold** can be found in the glossary on page 24.

Book Life
King's Lynn
Norfolk PE30 4LS

ISBN: 978-1-910512-95-1

©This edition was published in 2018. First published in 2016.

All rights reserved.
Printed in Malaysia.

A catalogue record for this book is available from the British Library.

Written by:
Grace Jones

Designed by:
Matt Rumbelow

Diwali

Festivals Around the World

Hello, my name is Prita.

When you see Prita, she will tell you how to say a word.

What Is a Festival?

A festival takes place when people come together to celebrate a special event or time of the year. Some festivals last for only one day and others can go on for many months.

Some people celebrate festivals by having a party with their family and friends. Others celebrate by holding special events, performing dances or playing music.

What Is Hinduism?

Hinduism is a **religion** that began in India over 4,000 years ago. Hindus believe in one god called **Brahman**. They pray to many different gods and goddesses who they believe are all forms of Brahman.

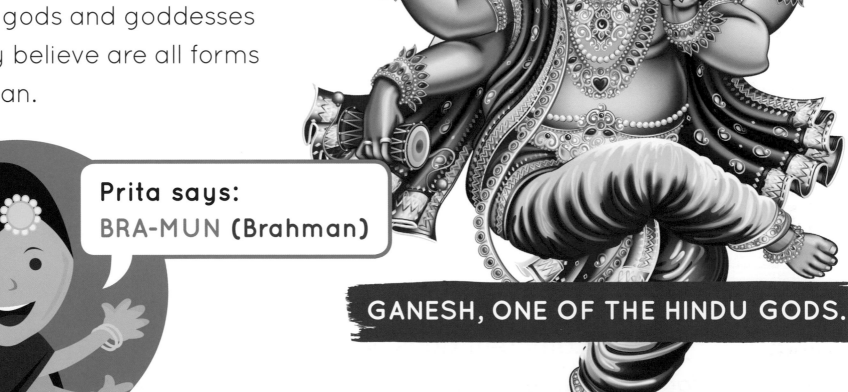

Prita says:
BRA-MUN (Brahman)

GANESH, ONE OF THE HINDU GODS.

Hindus pray to their different gods and goddesses in a temple, called a mandir. Before they enter a mandir, each person must wash so they are clean and remove their shoes as a sign of respect to God.

What Is Diwali?

Diwali is a festival that is celebrated by Hindus in October or November every year.

A HINDU TEMPLE IN MADURAI, INDIA.

Diwali celebrations usually last for five days.

The word Diwali means 'festival of lights'.

Hindus come together to celebrate the start of the new year. They celebrate by decorating their homes with many lights, exchanging gifts and setting off fireworks.

The Story of Diwali

A long, long time ago in India, there once was a prince called Rama who was married to a beautiful princess, Sita. Rama had an evil stepmother who wanted her son to become king instead of Rama. She sent Rama and Sita away to live in the forest.

Ravana, the demon king, had heard of Sita's great beauty. One day, he came to the forest and took her far away to his island. Rama was sad and did not know what to do. He asked the king of the monkeys, Hanuman, for help. They made a plan to rescue Sita.

Rama and Hanuman went to Ravana's island to find Sita. They found Ravana and fought with him for ten days. Rama shot a golden arrow that hit and finally killed Ravana. Rama and Sita were together once more.

Ravana had ten heads.

To learn how to say these words, look on page 22.

Rama and Sita tried to find their way home, but it was too dark. To help them, the people of the kingdom lit oil lamps so they could see. Rama and Sita finally came home and took their rightful place as king and queen.

Festival of Lights

At the beginning of Diwali, Hindus light small oil lamps to remember the story of Rama's **faith** in God and good winning over evil.

The small candles lit at Diwali are called diyas.

Diya

In the evening, big firework displays
are held, and people light sparklers and
lamps to celebrate Diwali. The fireworks
are thought to keep evil spirits away.

Prayer

In the evenings, many people hold a small prayer meeting called a puja. They pray to the god **Ganesh** and the goddess **Lakshmi**. Ganesh is the god of wisdom and good luck, and Lakshmi is the goddess of wealth and good fortune.

Lakshmi

Ganesh

Prita says:
LUK-SHMEE (Lakshmi)
GU-NESH (Ganesh)

Hindus also go to the mandir to **worship** Ganesh and Lakshmi. They give offerings of fruit and **traditional** Indian sweets to bring them good luck in the new year.

A Hindu temple in India.

Rangoli Decorations

People decorate the doorsteps of their houses and the ground outside the temples with brightly coloured patterns. These are called **Rangoli** patterns. They make them with a mixture of rice flour, water and coloured powder.

A Rangoli Pattern

Hindus hope the goddess Lakshmi will visit their houses when she sees the beautiful patterns. They believe she will bring them wealth and good luck in the new year.

Prita says:
LUK-SHMEE (Lakshmi)
RAN-GO-LEE (Rangoli)

THE HINDU GODDESS, LAKSHMI.

Festive Food

On the fourth day of Diwali, brothers visit their sisters for a special meal. Traditional festival foods, especially sweets, are eaten at this time of year.

Indian sweets are called mithai.

Mithai

Coconut **barfi** are especially popular during Diwali. They are small sweets made from coconut, milk and sugar.

Prita says:
CO-CO-NUT BAR-FEE (Coconut Barfi)

Music and Dancing

People fill the streets with lively dancing, to celebrate Diwali together as a community. A traditional stick dance, called the Dandiya Raas, is performed at this special time.

Traditional instruments, like the **dholak**, are played when performers are dancing. A dholak is a traditional hand drum. People also blow whistles and sing during the festival.

Prita says:
DO-LUK (Dholak)

Prita Says...

Brahman

Prita says "BRA-MUN"

The true Hindu God.

Coconut Barfi

Prita says "CO-CO-NUT BAR-FEE"

Small sweets made from coconut,
milk and sugar.

Dholak

Prita says "DO-LUK"

A traditional hand drum.

Ganesh

Prita says "GU-NESH"

The god of wisdom and good luck.

Hanuman

Prita says "HA-NOO-MUN"

The king of the monkeys.

Lakshmi

Prita says "LUK-SHMEE"

The goddess of wealth and good fortune.

Rangoli

Prita says "RAN-GO-LEE"

A colourful pattern drawn during Diwali.

Ravana

Prita says "RA-VARN-A"

The demon king.

Glossary

faith belief in a god(s).

religion a set of beliefs based around a god(s).

traditional something that is passed from person to person over a long time.

worship a religious act, such as praying.

Index

Photo Credits

Photocredits: Abbreviations: l-left, r-right, b-bottom, t-top, c-centre, m-middle. All images are courtesy of Shutterstock.com. Front Coverl — szefei. Front Coverr - wong sze yuen. 2 - India Picture. 4 - Tom Wang. 5 - imagedb.com. 6 - Tatyana Prokofieva. 7 - LiliGraphie. 8 - Noradoa. 9 - Mukesh Kumar. 10 - RoyStudio.eu. 10 l&r stockillustration. 11 - stockillustration. 12 - Tukaram Karve. 13 - aimy27feb. 14 - D.Shashikant. 15 - saiko3p. 16 - India Picture. 17 - Kudryashka. 18 - highviews. 19 - Swapan Photography. 20 - India Picture. 21 - imagedb.com.